SNOWY SCIENCE

**Shar Levine and
Leslie Johnstone**

25 Cool Experiments

**illustrations by
Patricia Storms**

SCHOLASTIC CANADA LTD.

Toronto New York London Auckland Sydney
Mexico City New Delhi Hong Kong Buenos Aires

Scholastic Canada Ltd.
604 King Street West, Toronto, Ontario M5V 1E1, Canada

Scholastic Inc.
557 Broadway, New York, NY 10012, USA

Scholastic Australia Pty Limited
PO Box 579, Gosford, NSW 2250, Australia

Scholastic New Zealand Limited
Private Bag 94407, Botany, Manukau 2163, New Zealand

Scholastic Children's Books
Euston House, 24 Eversholt Street, London NW1 1DB, UK

For Rachel Hauser of NCAR for setting up interviews, organizing a terrific fellowship, and driving me to really cool places in Boulder. Keep up the great work!
—SL

For my ski buddies: Janice, Ron, Megan, and Shar. Let's keep schussing!
—LJ

Acknowledgements
Thanks to Charles Knight and Teri Eastburn from the National Center for Atmospheric Research, for their advice, assistance, and information on all things frozen and winter.

Library and Archives Canada Cataloguing in Publication

Levine, Shar, 1953-
Snowy science : 25 cool experiments / Shar Levine and
Leslie Johnstone ; illustrations by Scholastic Canada Ltd.

Includes index.
ISBN 978-1-4431-0708-2

1. Winter--Experiments--Juvenile literature.
2. Cold--Experiments--Juvenile literature.
3. Science--Experiments--Juvenile literature.
I. Johnstone, Leslie II. Storms, Patricia III. Title.

QB637.8.L48 2011   j507.8   C2011-902460-8

6 5 4 3 2 1   Printed in Canada 118   11 12 13 14 15

FSC
www.fsc.org

MIX
Paper from
responsible sources
FSC® C011825

Table of Contents

Introduction

Good news: it's a snow day and there's no school. Bad news: it's a snow day . . . so what are you going to do for fun? How about doing some really cool science that can be done in very cool temperatures?

You might think that there isn't much science that can be done in winter. Unlike summer, when plants are growing and insects are buzzing around, winter doesn't seem to have much natural life to observe. But this season is one of the most fascinating times to perform experiments that might help you understand weather, climate change and the environment.

In this book you will learn that there's more to snow than just being white and fluffy. You will discover why frost forms in pretty patterns, how glaciers move and what causes avalanches.

So don't despair about the weather. Put on some warm clothes and get ready to have fun!

NOTE TO PARENTS AND TEACHERS

Snowy Science is a book that children of all ages will love. It will give children and adults an opportunity to see the connections between science and weather. Children learn best while they are having a good time. They will be fascinated to learn about snowflakes and may even enjoy the cold more when they discover they can make their own frozen treats using ice or snow.

Teachers can use this book as part of a lesson plan on weather or on the science of water, ice and snow. A fun activity that can be done indoors can be to chart the weather, record temperatures and even do some science from your window.

So grab a hot cup of cocoa, plop in some marshmallows and get ready for gales of laughter. There's more to winter than shovelling the sidewalks and wearing warm clothes.

SAFETY FIRST!

It's great to have fun and experiment, but there are some very simple rules to follow. If you aren't sure if something is all right to do, ask an adult.

DOS

1. Ask an adult before going outside to perform any experiments.
2. Before venturing outdoors, make certain you are wearing clothes that are appropriate for the weather conditions.
3. Tell an adult if you or anyone else is hurt in any way, or if any of your exposed body parts — nose, toes, fingers or ears — has **frostbite**.
4. Wear warm clothes, especially a hat, gloves, lined boots, scarf and winter pants and jacket. If you get wet, go inside and put on dry clothes.
5. Read all the steps of an experiment carefully, assemble your equipment, and be sure you know what to do before you begin an activity.
6. Always put away the materials you have used during the activities.
7. Stay in areas that are safe and approved by an adult.
8. If you get cold, come indoors immediately.

DON'TS

1. Do not go outdoors during a blizzard, ice storm or weather that is too cold or dangerous.
2. Do not use your bare hands to touch anything metal when outdoors during cold weather. Use gloves or mittens.
3. Do not eat, taste or lick anything unless the experiment says it is okay to do so. Before eating anything, ask an adult's permission.
4. Do not climb on huge snowbanks or play near roads.
5. Do not stand below icicles or in areas below snow-covered rooftops.

TIP: Some activities in this book call for you to crush ice. To do this, you can have an adult put ice in a sealable plastic bag, then smash it with a hammer. You can also put the ice in a sock and smash the sock against the sidewalk repeatedly.

WHY IS IT SO COLD IN WINTER?

A lot of people think that winters are cold because Earth is farther away from the sun. But that's not true. In fact, in the northern hemisphere where Canada is, we're closest to the sun in winter!

Earth revolves around, or circles, the sun — each circle takes a year. As it goes around the sun, Earth also rotates, or turns, every 24 hours, giving us our nights and our days. Over the course of the year, the distance between Earth and the sun does change, but not by very much. The seasons actually change because of the way Earth is *tilted* as it revolves around the sun.

On the part of the Earth that is tilted *away* from the sun, the sun's rays hit at an angle and the days are shorter. This makes it colder, giving us winter. The part tilted *toward* the sun gets more direct sunlight, longer days, warmer weather and summer. At the equator, which is the halfway point between the northern and southern hemispheres, the angle doesn't change as much, so it is warm there all year.

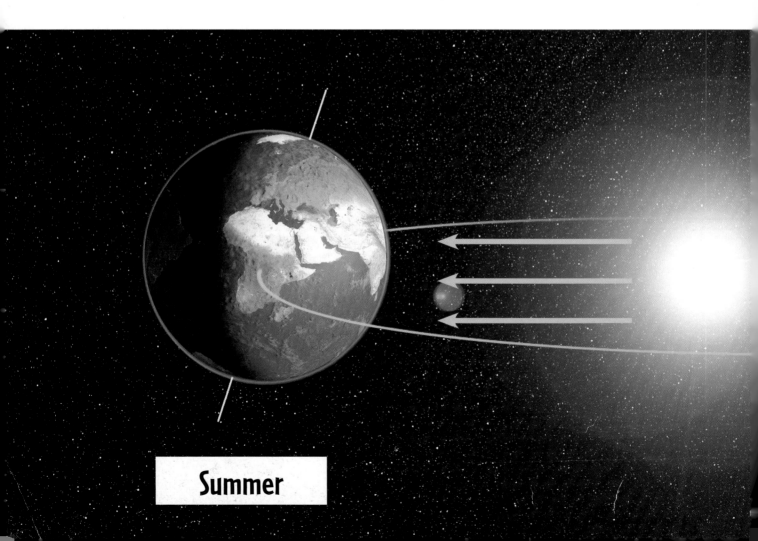

Summer

More light each day and more direct light due to the smaller angle are what make summer warm. Winter is colder because the days are shorter and the sunlight falls at a greater angle. In the southern hemisphere the angles are reversed, so it is summer there when it is winter in the north. At the equator the angle doesn't change as much so it is warm there year-round. At the poles there are days when it is either light or dark for 24 hours each day.

DID YOU KNOW?

The coldest temperature ever recorded in Canada is also the coldest temperature ever recorded in North America. It was −62.8°C (−81°F) on February 3, 1947 at Snag, Yukon.

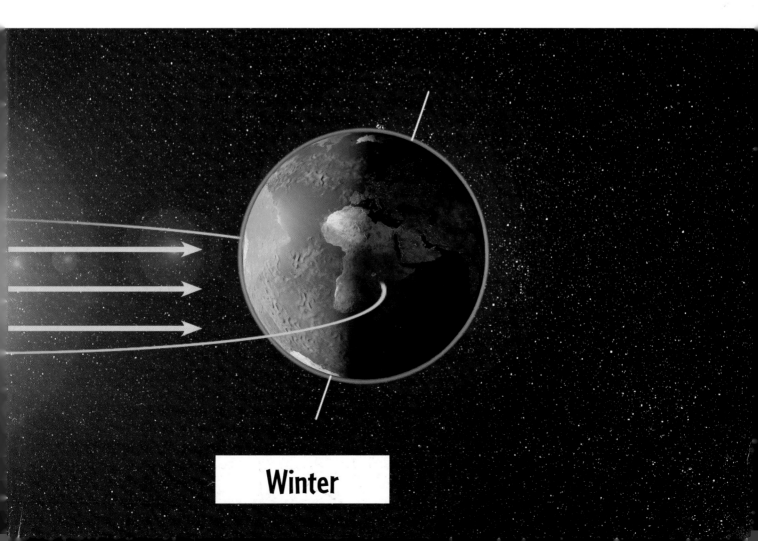

Winter

WHAT IS SNOW?

Snowflakes form as **water vapour** freezes into tiny **crystals**. These crystals can join together as more water freezes to make larger snowflakes. Snowflakes all look a little bit different, but they do have some things in common. Let's examine some snowflakes!

You Will Need

- a snowy day
- a small piece of black velvet, felt or other dark material
- a magnifying glass
- a freezer

What to Do

1. Place the black material in your freezer for at least 40 minutes.
2. On a snowy day, take the material out of the freezer just before you go outside. Lay the material flat on the ground or on a ledge and allow snowflakes to fall on the material.
3. Use a magnifying glass to study the snowflakes. What do they look like?
4. Try this again during a different snowstorm. Did the flakes look the same as in the first snowstorm?

WHAT HAPPENED?

All the snowflakes you examined had something in common: they all had six sides. All snowflakes have six sides, but different shapes. As extremely cold water falls from the clouds, it attaches to a dust particle and turns into an ice crystal. The crystals have flat six-sided (hexagonal) structures, giving snowflakes their special shape. The size and weight of a snowflake are affected by the temperature of the air, the amount of moisture in the cloud and other things like pollution. When it is is very cold you will see snow as individual flakes. When it is warmer, snow has some liquid water that makes it clump together.

KEEPING SNOWFLAKES

Now that you've caught some snowflakes, how can you keep them? Your parents probably won't be happy to have their freezer filled with snowballs made in the name of science, but they might appreciate having a piece of snowflake art.

You Will Need

- a clear CD jewel case
- aerosol hairspray (not the pump kind)
- a freezer
- a snowy day
- a magnifying glass

What to Do

1. Place the clean, empty CD jewel case in the freezer and the hairspray in the fridge overnight.
2. On the next snowy day, (preferably one with big flakes), just before you go outside, take the jewel case and hairspray from the fridge and freezer.
3. When you are outside, open the CD jewel case and spray the inside cover of the case with hairspray. Hold the jewel case flat and open to the falling snow.
4. Collect several flakes of snow on the sprayed plastic cover and then carefully close the case. Leave the case outside overnight in a safe place where it won't be disturbed as the hairspray hardens.
5. The next day, bring the jewel case inside and use a magnifying glass to look at the shapes of the flakes you captured.
6. Try this again on a day that the snowfall is different. Do different kinds of snowstorms make larger or smaller snowflakes?

WHAT HAPPENED?

The hairspray formed a shell around the snowflake. When the hairspray hardened, it preserved the shape of the flake. What kind of snowflake did you see?

HEAVY SNOWFALL

If you've ever shovelled snow, or tried to make a snow fort or snowball, you know that not all snow is the same. Powder snow that is light and airy doesn't make very good snowballs but is easy to move by the shovelful. Lifting slushy snow can feel like shovelling concrete. What is it that makes some snow heavier than others?

You Will Need

- a 250 mL (1 cup) measuring cup
- water
- snow
- a sealable plastic bag
- a pen and paper
- a kitchen scale
- measuring spoons

What to Do

1. Fill the measuring cup with 250 mL (1 cup) of water, and then pour the water in a sealable plastic bag. Place the sealed bag on the kitchen scale and weigh it. Record the weight of the bag of water. Reuse this bag for the next steps.
2. Fill the measuring cup with snow. Do not press the snow into the cup; just scoop it into the cup. Place the snow in the sealable plastic bag and weigh the sealed bag. Record the weight of the bag with the snow.
3. Fill the measuring cup again with snow, but this time add 4 tbsps of water to make 250 mL (1 cup) of slush. Place the snow slush into the sealable plastic bag and weigh the sealed bag. Record the weight of the bag with the slush.
4. Fill the measuring cup with snow, but this time pack the snow into the cup. Place the snow into the sealable plastic bag and weigh this. Record this weight.

WHAT HAPPENED?

Even though you had the same volume of material, you found that not all kinds of snow weighed the same. The freshly fallen, unpacked snow weighed the least. This was because it had air that took up space in the container. Air doesn't weigh nearly as much as snow or water. Light snow may only have a water content (the amount of water in each flake) of 1%, while wet snow may have a water content of 40%. Water is, of course, 100% water, which makes it very heavy. When the snow was compacted or pushed down, it weighed more than the fresh snow. The weight of snow is an important thing to know, especially if you are putting a roof or deck on your house. People want to make sure that the structure they have built won't collapse under the weight of a heavy snowfall or ice storm.

DID YOU KNOW?

It is often said that no two snowflakes are alike. But in 1988 scientist Nancy Knight of the National Center for Atmospheric Research in Boulder Colorado found two flakes that, for the most part, seemed to be identical.

MEASURING SNOW

There was a huge snowstorm last night, and this morning everything is covered in a white blanket of snow . . . but did enough snow fall so that school will be cancelled? Other than turning on the TV or checking the Internet to find out how much snow fell, is there a way to measure snowfall?

You Will Need

- a snowy day
- a large empty coffee can or similar sized container
- a ruler
- masking tape
- duct tape (optional)
- a stick or spatula
- a large measuring cup, 500 mL (2 cups) or larger

What to Do

1. Place a ruler inside the coffee can and tape it securely to one side with your masking tape. This is your snow gauge.
2. When it starts to snow, put the gauge outside, in an open area, away from trees and buildings. If you want, you can use duct tape to attach the gauge to a fence post. If you are putting the snow gauge on the ground, you might want to place a few rocks around the gauge so that it doesn't blow over.
3. When it has stopped snowing, bring the gauge inside. Use a stick or a spatula to take off any snow that is covering the rim of the can. Check your ruler to see how much snow you collected.
4. Leave the gauge in a warm place and allow the snow to melt. Pour it in the measuring cup. How much water was there compared to the snow level?

WHAT HAPPENED?

Your snow gauge collected the snow that fell over a period of time. This gives you an idea of how many centimetres or inches of snow fell in your area. You were also able to compare the amount of snow to the amount of water.

DID YOU KNOW?

There are several ways of classifying or describing snowflakes. There is even an "International Classification System," which was created by the International Commission on Snow. This system identifies seven shapes: plates, stellar crystals, columns, needles, spatial dendrites, capped columns and irregular forms.

WE ALL SCREAM FOR SNOW CREAM

There are a great many myths surrounding the invention of ice cream. Some claim that Italian explorer Marco Polo brought back the secret of ice cream from his travels to China, where they had been making frozen desserts for thousands of years. No one is sure if this is really true, but what is true is that science plays a big role in the creation of this fabulous dessert.

You Will Need

- an adult helper
- a small sealable plastic bag
- a large sealable plastic bag
- 125 mL (½ cup) whipping cream
- 125 mL (½ cup) half and half cream
- 2 mL (½ tsp) vanilla flavouring
- 5 mL (1 tsp) sugar
- 75 mL (¼ cup) of your favourite chocolate chips or small bits of fresh berries, like blueberries or strawberries
- fresh snow or crushed ice from your freezer
- a fridge
- salt
- mittens or gloves

NOTE: If you can't drink milk, you can use almond milk, coconut milk, rice milk or soy milk instead of cream.

What to Do

1. Ask an adult helper to approve of all the ingredients to ensure that you can eat the ingredients in this experiment.
2. Pour the liquid ingredients into the small bag and add in the sugar, crumbled bits of chocolate treats or fresh fruit. Squeeze out most of the air and then tightly seal the bag. Leave this in the fridge for several hours.
3. Take the small bag from the fridge and place it inside the large plastic bag. Fill the large bag with snow or ice, leaving enough room so that you can seal it. Pour about 250 mL (1 cup) of salt over the snow or ice, then seal the outer plastic bag. The salty slush you have created is called **brine**.

4. Put on your mittens or gloves and, holding the bag very tightly, begin to shake and rock the bag back and forth. If you get tired shaking the bag, take turns with a friend.
5. Be patient. It can take about 20 minutes for the liquid to freeze and turn into ice cream.

WHAT HAPPENED?

You made ice cream! Pure water freezes or turns into ice at 0˚C (32˚F). Adding salt to ice water causes it to have a lower **freezing point**. Placing the cooled cream mixture into the extra-cold brine caused the cream to begin to form ice and fat crystals. Shaking the bag made the ice cream smoother by adding some air into the mixture.

SNOW WHITE...
WITHOUT THE DWARFS

Water from the tap is clear — or it should be. Ice is transparent. So why is snow white? Why do glaciers look blue?

You Will Need

- a helper
- 3 flashlights
- red, green and blue cellophane or plastic filters
- 3 rubber bands
- a white wall or large piece of white paper

What to Do

1. Cover the glass or clear plastic end (the part over the bulb) of one of the flashlights with the red cellophane. Wrap a rubber band around the rim to secure it. Cover the end of the second flashlight with the green cellophane and secure it with the rubber band around the rim. Cover the third flashlight with the blue cellophane and secure it with a rubber band.
2. Have a friend turn on the red flashlight and shine it against a white wall or large piece of white paper. You should have a circle of red light.
3. Shine the green flashlight so that the beam of light overlaps one edge of the red light. What colour do you see where they overlap?
4. Shine the blue flashlight so that the beam of light overlaps the green and red circles of light. What colour do you see where all three beams of light overlap?

16

WHAT HAPPENED?

The spot where all three beams of light met was white. The spot where the blue and green met was turquoise, and where the red and blue beam met was purple. The red and green light combined to make yellow. You used red, green and blue cellophane because these are additive primary colours. Now what does this have to do with snow? When water freezes into ice it isn't perfectly transparent — it bends light a little bit. This is called **refraction**. The ice acts like a prism and can make the light different colours. Snow is made up of lots of ice crystals. When light hits snowflakes, the light is bent several different ways at once and the result is that all the colours of light that come out get blended and the snow looks white.

DID YOU KNOW?

In what must have been a very odd storm, orange snow fell in a large area around Siberia, Russia, on February 2, 2007. Scientists believe that a sand storm in Kazakhstan combined with a snowstorm in Siberia turning the snow a sandy colour.

INSTANT ICE

Charles Knight, of the University Corporation for Atmospheric Research in Boulder, Colorado, in the United States, has one *very* cool lab. Really, really cool. He has a sub-zero cold room with a do-it-yourself cloud chamber, where he studies snow and ice crystals. Although you may not be able to perform some of his experiments at home, you can try this one.

You Will Need

- an adult helper
- 250 mL (1 cup) distilled water from a pharmacy or grocery store (not tap water or boiled water)
- a clean, smooth drinking glass (the glass must have straight sides and not have any patterns, indentations or flaws; do not use a plastic jar or cup)
- a large plastic container
- crushed ice
- 500 mL (2 cups) table salt
- an outdoor thermometer

What to Do

1. Pour the distilled water into the clean glass.
2. Place the glass into the plastic container. Add enough crushed ice to the container so that it goes past the level of the water in the jar.
3. Carefully pour the salt over the ice. Do not get any salt into the water in the glass.
4. Place the outdoor thermometer into the water. Wait about 20 minutes.
5. When the temperature of the water in the glass reaches –1°C (30°F), take the thermometer out of the glass. Have an adult carefully remove the glass from the ice by lifting it straight up. This should be done in a smooth motion so that the water in the glass does not move.
6. Place the glass on a counter top. Take a small piece of crushed ice (a fresh piece, not one that was in the ice mixture) and drop it into the water.

WHAT HAPPENED?

When the chip of ice touched the cold water, crystals began to form and the water turned into ice. The water had been cooled below the freezing point, but still hadn't frozen. That's because if water is cooled quickly to just below the freezing point (you did this by adding the salt), it can still stay liquid, but supercooled. Ice crystals need to have somewhere to form. A speck of dirt or sand will do, or even a scratch on the glass water container. The ice you added acted as a seed crystal which helped the ice grow, and the cold water immediately began to freeze.

DEEP FREEZE

After an early frost, the flowers in your garden may droop and leaves on certain plants lie on the ground. Other plants don't appear to have changed at all. Why do some plants live through the winter while others die?

You Will Need

- several fresh green peas (shelled)
- several fresh strawberries
- grapes
- a slice of bread
- a potato slice
- a lettuce leaf
- a melon slice
- a cookie sheet
- a freezer

What to Do

1. Place the peas, strawberries, grapes, bread, potato, lettuce and melon on the cookie sheet, leaving space between the items so they do not touch.
2. Put the cookie sheet into the freezer and leave it overnight or until all the items are completely frozen.
3. Remove the cookie sheet from the freezer and allow the items to thaw. What do they look like?

WHAT HAPPENED?

Some items like the strawberries, melon and lettuce turned soft and mushy after they thawed. These items have a high water content or a lot of water in their **cells**. As the water froze, it expanded and burst the cells. When thawed, there was nothing to help the item keep its shape. The potato and bread did not contain as much water, so they kept their shape and texture after they thawed. Grapes and peas kept their shape because they have a skin that contains less water than their inner flesh, which is mushy.

QUINZHEE

An **igloo** is a dwelling built with cut blocks of frozen snow. Like an igloo, a **quinzhee** (pronounced KWIN-zee) is also an outdoor dwelling made of snow, but it is a more like a snow cave. Let's build a small one and use it for an experiment.

You Will Need

- an adult helper
- a thick snow pile
- two ski or insulated mittens
- a hair dryer
- duct tape
- two outdoor thermometers at room temperature

What to Do

1. After a heavy snowfall where there is about 30 cm (1 ft) of new snow on the ground, look for a deep snow pile with fresh, light snow. This should be away from a driveway or street. A snow-covered balcony or table would be perfect.
2. Select the snow pile where you want to put one of the mittens. Punch a hole into the side of the snow pile up to about your elbow.
3. Go back inside and use the hair dryer to warm the inside of the mittens. These will represent your body. Place one thermometer into each ski mitten. Tape the end of each mitten shut. Attach a long piece of duct tape to the ends of each mitten.
4. Quickly run outside with the mittens. Place one of the mittens inside the hole in the snow. The duct tape should dangle out of the hole so you can find the mitten. Immediately cover the hole with snow. Place the second mitten outside the hole, on top of the snow. Leave the mittens undisturbed for 15 minutes.
5. Check the temperature of the thermometer that was outside of the snow cave. What is the temperature? Pull gently on the duct tape to retrieve the buried mitten and check the temperature.

WHAT HAPPENED?

The mitten that was in the quinzhee wasn't as cold as the mitten that was left on top of the snow. That's because snow kept the inside of your quinzhee from getting too cold. Snow acts as an **insulator** because it is filled with trapped air. As much as 95% of the volume of freshly fallen snow can be air. The trapped air prevents heat from leaving the quinzhee and keeps the air inside warmer than the outside air. Outdoor enthusiasts who have slept overnight in a larger version of this snow hut report that no matter how cold and windy it was outside, the temperature inside was a balmy –2°C (28°F). That may not seem too warm, but if the temperature outside of the snow hut was –40°C (–40°F), it would probably keep you from freezing to death (presuming you had a warm sleeping bag and winter clothing on).

DID YOU KNOW?

People wear glasses with polarized or special lenses to protect their eyes from the damaging rays of the sun. But did you know that you also need these glasses in the winter? Bright, white snow reflects the ultraviolet light rays from the sun. That glare can cause a temporary condition called **snow blindness**. In the Arctic, the Inuit used to make a type of goggle by putting thin slits in masks made from caribou antlers and tying them around their heads with sinew straps.

SLIP SLIDING AWAY

When an **avalanche** strikes, it looks like a wave of snow rushing down a slope, carrying with it rocks, trees, ice and just about anything in its path. Avalanches can be very dangerous to people who hike or ski in remote areas, easily burying them. Let's try creating one on a much smaller scale.

You Will Need

- a helper
- newspapers or an old bed sheet
- a large piece of corrugated cardboard about 60 cm by 90 cm (2 ft by 3 ft)
- a pencil
- a ruler
- aluminum foil
- an old T-shirt
- different kinds of sandpaper (used sandpaper is fine)
- a glue stick
- scissors
- a sieve or flour sifter
- pebbles
- sugar or table salt
- flour
- mashed potato flakes
- cornstarch (optional)
- a large, flat metal spatula
- a protractor

What to Do

1. Gather the materials you need. Spread the newspapers or bed sheet on the ground. Lay your cardboard flat on this surface.
2. Measure the long side of the cardboard rectangle. Use the ruler and divide the cardboard into 4 equal columns.
3. Cut the aluminum foil and old T-shirt to fit within a column.
4. Use the glue stick and attach the aluminum foil to one column. Leave the next column without any material. Use the glue stick to attach the T-shirt strip to the third column. Glue large sections of the sandpaper to the last column. If you wish, you can glue small rocks over the sandpaper section. These are your **terrains** or ground covers.
5. Sprinkle all four columns with a light dusting of sugar or salt. Use the spatula to press down the sugar.
6. Place enough flour over the sugar to completely cover the sugar. To get an even cover, use a sieve or flour sifter to shake the flour over the sugar. Use the spatula to press down the flour.
7. Sprinkle the top of the flour with potato flakes. Use the spatula to press this layer down.
8. If you wish, give another light dusting of flour or cornstarch on top of the potato flakes. This is your mountain. Each of the layers represents a **snowpack**.

9. Have your helper hold the protractor upright at the end of one of the short sides (the bottom of your mountain). The centre of the protractor should be even with the corner of the cardboard.
10. Slowly lift the top of the mountain (the end away from the protractor). Watch what happens to the snow on the mountain. To what angle can you lift the mountain before things begin to slide? Which terrain has an avalanche first? Which one has one last? Note the different angles.
11. Gather up all the food materials and dispose of them in the garbage or compost.

WHAT HAPPENED?

Each layer represents a kind of snowpack created by a storm on the mountain. Several snowstorms might hit a mountain during the winter season, leaving light, wet or icy snow that gets packed down by the weight of the new layers of snow on top. The columns represent different mountain terrains. The kind of terrain or ground cover affects the way that snow sticks to the surface of the mountain. The rougher the terrain, the less the snow slid. The smoother the terrain, the easier it was for snow to slide off of the mountain. The protractor showed you how the steepness of the mountain can also affect how easy it is for an avalanche to start.

DID YOU KNOW?

There are several new life-saving devices that can help people survive avalanches. One is a backpack that inflates, providing a cushion of air around the head of the user. It also has a global positioning system (GPS) device to help rescuers find the trapped skier.

MAKE YOUR OWN GLACIER

Some parts of the world have winter weather year-round. It may not actually be winter, but these locations are cold and have long-lasting sheets of ice and snow called **glaciers**. Glaciers form when more snow falls than melts each year. If you've ever made a snowball, you know that snow sticks together when you squeeze it. In the same way you make a snowball, the years of thawing, squeezing and freezing causes glaciers to become massive sheets of ice made up of different layers. Let's look at how the layers of ice on top squeeze the ice at the bottom.

You Will Need
- a narrow, straight-sided drinking glass
- a piece of light cardboard
- a pencil
- scissors
- marshmallows
- rolls of pennies

What to Do

1. Place the drinking glass or jar upside down on the piece of light cardboard. Use a pencil to trace a circle around the rim of the glass.
2. Use scissors to cut out a circle slightly smaller than the one you traced on the cardboard. Your cardboard circle should fit loosely inside the glass.
3. Place enough marshmallows in a glass to almost fill it to the rim. Cover the stack of marshmallows with the cardboard circle.
4. Add your roll of pennies and watch what happens.
5. Add additional weights to see how the stack changes with more weight. See what happens when you remove the weights.

WHAT HAPPENED?

The marshmallows became shorter and fatter until they came in contact with the sides of the glass or jar. The more weight you added, the more the marshmallows shortened and flattened. The marshmallows on the bottom were a bit thinner than those at the top. Depending on how fresh your marshmallows were you may have found that they didn't spring right back into the original shape when the pressure was released, but stayed stuck together and flattened. This is similar to how glaciers are formed as the snow, like your marshmallows, packs down over time. The weight on the top, combined with years of thawing and freezing, forms denser layers of ice at the bottom of the glacier.

DID YOU KNOW?

Glaciers hold about two-thirds of the fresh water on Earth. If all the glaciers were to melt, Earth's oceans would rise by more than 70 m (230 ft), enough to flood cities along the coastline. You would find water as high as the 22nd floor in buildings that were originally at sea level.

MOVING GLACIER

When they are moving, glaciers act like massive rivers of ice that slide slowly along in the bed they have carved out over thousands of years. Glaciers can move up to 200 metres (656 ft) each year. Glaciers can move at different speeds depending on the local conditions. What has to happen to make the glacier travel more rapidly down a slope? When are they most likely to move slowly? We can't travel to a glacier, but we can use some slimy putty to make our own glacier moving model.

You Will Need

- an adult helper
- aluminum foil
- cooking oil
- 2 sealable plastic bags
- food colouring

- 125 mL (½ cup) white glue
- hand cream
- 150 mL (⅔ cup) warm water
- 5 mL (1 tsp) borax

- a piece of corrugated cardboard, at least 30 cm (1 ft) long
- sandpaper
- a ruler

Note: Borax can make you sick if you swallow it, so this experiment is not for younger children who might try to taste it. After handling the putty, be sure to wash your hands with soap and water.

What to Do

1. Fold the cardboard along the corrugation so it forms a right angle. This is your valley.
2. Line the valley with a piece of aluminum foil. Cover the foil with a thin layer of cooking oil.
3. Pour the glue into a plastic bag. Add a drop of food colouring and a drop of hand cream. Seal the bag and squeeze the goo to mix it.

4. Put the warm water into a second bag and have an adult add the borax and seal the bag. Shake to mix.
5. Pour about 30 mL (2 tbsp) of the borax mixture into the bag of goo. Close the bag and squeeze the mixture.
6. Pour the rest of the borax liquid into the bag of goo. Seal the bag and knead until you have a solid blob. Now it is ready for the experiment. Take it out of the bag and hold it in your hand. It should start to flow through your fingers. See what happens if you pinch a bit of it and pull on it sharply.
7. Place the blob of slimy putty at one end of the valley and lift that end until the putty starts to slide. Measure the height of the end of the valley with the ruler.
8. Try this again with the end of the valley at a greater height. What happens to the putty?
9. Remove the aluminum foil and try lining the valley with a piece of sandpaper. Repeat steps 7 and 8. How does the sandpaper affect the movement of the putty?

WHAT HAPPENED?

When you mixed together the ingredients and kneaded it, you made a runny plastic glob of slimy goo. Glaciers flowing down a slope under pressure act a bit like the goo. Rapid movement, like when you pinched off a piece of it, can cause a crack or break. In glaciers, these breaks are called crevasses and they are often seen as pieces of glaciers begin to break off near the ocean to form **icebergs**. When you made your valley steeper, the goo moved faster. The smooth surface and a layer of oil also made it move faster. Rough surfaces such as the sandpaper can slow the putty down due to friction. Glaciers will move faster down a smooth steep slope. If the glacier is melting at the bottom, the layer of water that forms can help speed it on its way.

DID YOU KNOW?

On August 5, 2010, a block of ice 183 m (600 ft) thick and about 260 square kilometres (100 square miles) broke off a glacier in Greenland. Scientists are alarmed at the number of large chunks that are breaking off glaciers around the world. They think that climate change is behind the disappearance, or shrinking, of glaciers.

JACK FROST

If you've ever gotten into a car that was parked outside on a very cold day, you may have noticed that the windows were covered with a layer of frozen water called **frost**, which develops when water in the air forms tiny solid crystals on surfaces near the ground. Here is a way to make your own frost.

You Will Need

- a metal container with a lid (empty coffee cans work well)
- ice cubes
- 125 mL (½ cup) salt
- paper
- 5 mL (1 tsp) water

What to Do

1. Add enough ice cubes to the metal container so that it is about ¾ full.
2. Add the salt to the ice cubes. Place the lid on the container and shake the container up and down for about 1 minute to mix the ice and salt together.
3. Place the piece of paper on a kitchen counter or other waterproof surface. Pour water over the top of the piece of paper.
4. Place the metal container on top of the piece of paper. Check the outside of the container every 10 minutes. Try blowing gently on the outside of the container to see what happens.

WHAT HAPPENED?

You made frost! The salt caused the ice to melt slightly, but it also made the melting temperature of the ice lower. Water vapour in the air froze on the cold surface of the container to form frost. If you blew gently on the container, you may have seen more frost because your breath has more water vapour in it than the air does. If you blew too hard or too close to the container, the warmth of your breath could have caused the frost to melt.

IT'LL GROW ON YOU

You can inflate a balloon by blowing more air into it. But how can you make water "larger" without any more liquid?

You Will Need

- a 500 mL (2 cup) plastic liquid measuring cup
- cold water
- plastic wrap
- a freezer

What to Do

1. Add exactly 250 mL (1 cup) of cold water to the measuring cup and cover the top of the cup with a piece of plastic wrap to seal.
2. Place the cup into the freezer and leave overnight.
3. Remove the cup after the water has frozen, remove the plastic wrap and check the level of the water against the measurements on the side of the cup.

WHAT HAPPENED?

You discovered that the water expanded or took up more space. Water is made up of billions of tiny particles called molecules. At first, the volume of the water shrank a little bit as the molecules moved closer together, until it reached 4°C (39°F). As it got colder something strange happened — the molecules began to move farther apart. This happened because the water molecules began to join together to form crystals. Once the water reached the freezing point, the molecules were locked in place at a set distance from each other. This made the volume of frozen water larger than the volume of cold water.

ICE TUBES

Studying **ice cores**, long tubes of ice that are drilled from the ground, is a way for scientists to look back in time and see what climate conditions were like thousands of years ago. The National Snow and Ice Data Center in Boulder, Colorado, in the United States studies the **cryosphere,** the parts of the Earth where water is frozen year-round. They take ice core samples from far below the Antarctic ice. You might not be able to drill deep into ice from the Antarctic, but you can get an idea of what ice cores might look like.

You Will Need

- an adult helper
- 4 identical round plastic containers, one with a lid
- masking tape
- boiled water
- a felt-tipped marker
- tap water

- distilled water from a pharmacy or grocery store
- carbonated water
- a 250mL (1 cup) measuring cup
- a freezer
- a cookie sheet
- a magnifying glass

What to Do

1. Place a piece of masking tape on the side of each container. Use the marker to label the containers: tap, distilled, carbonated, boiled.
2. Ask an adult to boil water and pour 250 mL (1 cup) into the appropriately labelled container. Place a lid on this container.
3. Measure the distilled water, tap water and carbonated water and pour 250 mL (1 cup) of each substance into the labelled containers.
4. Place all the containers in the freezer and leave overnight. These are your ice cores.
5. The next morning take the containers out of the freezer and turn them upside down on a cookie sheet, being careful to note which is which. Use a magnifying glass to closely examine each ice core. Do they look the same? Was there anything on the inside of the lid?
6. Stack the ice cores one on top of the other. Can you tell what kind of water made up each core?

WHAT HAPPENED?

Each core was different. The core made from carbonated water had bubbles frozen in the ice. The core from tap water was cloudy, while the one made from distilled water was clear. The core made from boiled water was also quite clear. The lid from the boiled water may have grown ice crystals. This is because the steam rising from the boiled water contained water vapour. The lid prevented the water vapour from escaping from the container, and it condensed or turned into drops of water. The cold temperature caused the water to freeze and turn into crystals. Tap water contains minerals and impurities, which make the ice cloudy, while the frozen distilled water is clear because it is only water.

DID YOU KNOW?

When **glaciologists,** or scientists that study glaciers, study ice cores, they do more than look at the bubbles or clarity of the ice. They can tell how much snow fell in a particular year. They also analyze chemicals, ash and other particles that can be found in the air. This helps them learn something about climate change and carbon dioxide levels.

ICE SPIKES

You have probably seen icicles dangling down from trees or the eaves of a house, but did you know ice can also grow upwards? Making ice spikes is an interesting experiment that will show you how ice freezes.

You Will Need

- distilled water from a pharmacy or grocery store
- a clean ice cube tray
- a freezer
- a small, battery-operated fan (optional)

What to Do

1. Pour a bit of distilled water into a clean ice cube tray, swirl it around and pour it out. This will ensure the tray is very clean.
2. Fill the ice cube tray with distilled water and place on a very flat surface in the freezer. Leave the freezer closed overnight. Don't peek.
3. Check on your tray the next day. Do you notice anything unusual about the cubes?
4. Allow the ice to melt in the tray then try this again, this time placing a small battery-operated fan close to the surface of the ice cube tray with the distilled water.

WHAT HAPPENED?

You grew tiny ice spikes on the surface of the cubes. Ice doesn't freeze all at once. Water first freezes on the surface, around the edges of what will become the ice cube, then in from the edges, until just a small hole is left unfrozen in the middle of the surface. Water is then pushed up through the hole and freezes in a spike. An unfrozen water droplet sits on the top and more water freezes around this spike. The spike gets taller until the tube finally freezes and closes.

ICE TRICK

Want to amaze your friends? Show them how to pick up an ice cube using just salt and a piece of string!

You Will Need

- a drinking glass
- water
- an ice cube
- string
- salt

What to Do

1. Fill a drinking glass about ¾ full of water. Add an ice cube.
2. Drape a piece of string over the top of the ice cube. Let it sit for two minutes then lift the string. What happened?
3. Drape the string over the top of the ice cube again. Shake some salt onto the top of the string and the ice cube. Wait for two minutes then try lifting the string again.

WHAT HAPPENED?

When you tried to lift the ice cube using the string the first time, it probably didn't work. The string wouldn't freeze to the ice. But when you added salt, it melted the ice (because salt lowers the freezing temperature of water) and stopped it from refreezing at the surface. The water underneath the string had less salt in it, so the colder temperature causes it to freeze around the string. And voila! You lifted the ice with a piece of string!

CUTTING ICE

It's easy to cut through a pile of snow, but ice can be hard to cut. How about cutting ice with a wire? Do you think it can be done? Let's find out!

You Will Need

- a 1 L (1 qt) milk carton
- scissors
- water
- a freezer

- a cookie sheet
- 2 kitchen chairs
- 1 m (1 yd) of fine copper wire
- two 1 L (1 qt) juice jugs with handles and lids

What to Do

1. Cut open one side of a milk carton to make a mold for a thick rectangular block of ice. Add about 2 cm (1 in) of water into the container and freeze it to make the ice block. When the ice is frozen, peel off the container to release the ice block.
2. Place the cookie sheet on the floor. Place two chairs so that the front legs are inside the cookie sheet. Carefully balance the ice block so it is held up by the seats of the chairs.
3. Wind the ends of the copper wire through the handles of the two juice containers leaving about 30 cm (1 ft) of wire between the two jugs. Fill the jugs with water and seal the lids.
4. Drape the wire across the piece of ice with one jug on each side. Let the jugs hang down underneath the ice.
5. Watch what happens as the wire cuts into the ice. What happens when the wire makes it through to the bottom of the ice block?

WHAT HAPPENED?

When the wire put pressure on the ice, it melted it and cut into the block. As the pressure of the wire came off, the water above the wire began to refreeze. Eventually the wire made its way completely through the ice block and fell onto the cookie sheet below. When this happened, the block of ice stayed together because enough of it had refrozen to join the block back together.

DID YOU KNOW?

Scientists used to believe that the pressure put onto ice by the thin blades of an ice skate melted the ice enough so the skate could glide along a layer of water. The only problem is that the ice skate blade doesn't put enough pressure on the ice for long enough to cause the ice to melt. Recent research shows that ice surfaces have a thin water-like layer of molecules that allow skates (and pucks) to slide easily along the surface.

DO-IT-YOURSELF ICEBERG

An iceberg is an enormous floating piece of freshwater ice that has broken off of a glacier. Most of an iceberg is below the waterline. You can make your own balloon icebergs.

You Will Need

- 3 balloons of different sizes
- water
- a freezer
- a large bucket
- ice cubes
- scissors
- a plastic ruler

What to Do

1. Blow up your balloons to stretch them before you begin. Then fill the balloons with water. Tie the ends of the balloons to seal them. These will be your icebergs.
2. Place the balloons in the freezer overnight.
3. Fill up the bucket with cold water, leaving a bit of space at the top for the water to rise when the balloons are added. Stir in a few ice cubes to cool the water down even more.
4. Remove the frozen balloons from the freezer. Use scissors to cut open the balloons and peel them off to remove your icebergs.
5. When the ice cubes in your bucket have melted, add your icebergs. Look to see how they float in the water. Measure the height of each iceberg above the water with a ruler and compare it to the icebergs' total height. Are there any differences between the balloons?

WHAT HAPPENED?

You made icebergs in your freshwater ocean. You used the height of the iceberg and not its mass (how much it weighs) to compare them and probably found that about $\frac{1}{8}$ of the height of each was above the water level. For real icebergs, the amount of ice above the ocean water can be anywhere from $\frac{1}{6}$ to $\frac{1}{9}$.

WATER RISING

Icebergs can range in size from as small as a car to the size of an island. But does the ocean rise as the icebergs melt? Here's one way to see what happens when icebergs melt.

You Will Need

- 2 identical clear plastic glasses
- a rock about the size of a D battery
- water
- a marker
- two large ice cubes

What to Do

1. Place the rock in the bottom of one glass. Add water to the glass to just cover the rock.
2. Add water to the second glass so it is at the same height as the water in the first one. Mark the water level on the side of each glass with a marker. Label this line "A."
3. Place one ice cube on top of the rock. Add the other ice cube to the second glass so it is floating in the water. Mark the water levels again. Label this line "B."
4. Leave the glasses for a few minutes until all of the ice has melted in each glass. Mark the new water levels on the glass. Label this line "C." Has the water level risen?

WHAT HAPPENED?

After the ice melted, the water level rose in the first cup but didn't change very much in the second cup. Placing the ice in the second cup had already changed the water level. Icebergs don't change the water level very much once they have already formed. Most of the change in water level happens when the ice enters the water as the iceberg **calves** from the glacier.

WIND CHILL

The weather report on the radio says that it is –10°C (14°F) outside today with a **wind chill** of –22°C (–8°F). What exactly does the weather reporter mean? How can the temperature have two different numbers? Well, really it doesn't. The temperature is –10°C, but because it is windy, it *feels* as if it is –22°C. The difference between the actual temperature and the way it feels is called wind chill. Let's look at how this works.

You Will Need

- a room thermometer
- an electric fan
- a mister or spray bottle of water

What to Do

1. Measure the temperature of the room.
2. Turn on the fan and stand in front of it. How does the wind from the fan make you feel? Measure the temperature in front of the fan.
3. Mist or spray your arm with water. Stand in front of the fan to see how the wind feels on your wet arm.
4. Mist the air in front of the fan and then measure the temperature in the area you misted.

WHAT HAPPENED?

You feel colder when you stand in front of the fan. The wind cools your skin, but the room temperature is unchanged. Even if you turn the fan up to a higher speed, it won't change the temperature. When you put water on your arm and stand in front of the fan, the evaporation of the water, as it changes from liquid water into water vapour, makes your skin feel colder. That's why it's important to stay dry when you're outside in cold and windy weather.

FROZEN FISH

Some fish live in oceans where the water temperature is below the freezing temperature of their blood. Why don't they freeze? It turns out that they have a group of very special antifreeze **proteins** in their blood. Scientists have studied the water molecules and the proteins in fish blood. They have discovered that these proteins change the way the water molecules move and prevent the water in the blood from forming crystals and freezing. You may not be able to make the special fish proteins found in fish that live in very cold water, but you can investigate how different liquids freeze.

You Will Need

- an adult helper
- a large bowl
- crushed ice
- 250 mL (1 cup) salt
- a large spoon
- 3 small glass jars with lids
- a marker
- water
- canola or grape seed cooking oil
- rubbing alcohol

Note: Rubbing alcohol can be poisonous if swallowed, so an adult helper should supervise this experiment and all the jars should be kept separate from food.

What to Do

1. Half fill a large bowl with crushed ice. Pour about 250 mL (1 cup) of salt over the ice and mix the ice and salt together well with the large spoon.
2. Label one glass jar "water," one jar "oil," and the final jar "alcohol."
3. Have an adult half fill each of the jars with the ingredient on the label and seal them.
4. Place the jars into the crushed ice bath. Watch to see what happens.

WHAT HAPPENED?

The cooking oil began to form a solid lump after a few minutes. You may also have seen some ice forming in the jar containing water. But no matter how cold your ice and salt mixture was, you wouldn't see the rubbing alcohol forming a solid. This is because the melting and freezing temperature of each of these liquids is different. If the liquid has a higher freezing point than the ice and salt mixture the liquid will freeze. Your ice and salt mixture is colder that the temperature at which the cooking oil freezes (around 10°C or 50°F). The water has a melting point of 0°C (32°F), which is also higher than the salt and ice. Only the rubbing alcohol, which freezes at about −89°C (−128°F), will remain a liquid.

DID YOU KNOW?

The *Rana sylvatica*, a wood frog commonly found in Canada, has an unusual ability: it can freeze solid with almost 65% of the creature turning into ice. When the weather gets warmer, it thaws and happily hops away.

KEEPING WARM

You can probably sit inside on a cold day and be quite comfortable, but people didn't always have warm homes in winter. Depending on where you live, it is likely that insulation, furnaces and other heating systems keep you warm in winter. In the summer, you may have air conditioning and refrigeration to keep things cool. Insulation is used to keep heat from leaving your house in the winter, but it also keeps heat from entering in the summer. Let's look at how this works.

You Will Need

- newspaper
- a coffee can or other large can with a lid
- two identical small plastic containers with lids
- two large ice cubes as close to the same size as possible

What to Do

1. Crumple up a sheet of newspaper and place it in the bottom of the coffee can.
2. Place one of the small containers on top of the crumpled newspaper. Crumple more newspaper and pack it in loosely around the small container.
3. Put an ice cube in each of the small containers. Place the lids on the containers.
4. Crumple additional newspaper and place it loosely on top of the first small container until the coffee can is full. Place the lid on the coffee can.
5. Put the coffee can and the second small container somewhere warm and leave them for 10 minutes. Remove the lids from the small containers and note how much of the ice has melted. Replace the lids.
6. Repeat step 4 several times until all the ice has melted.

WHAT HAPPENED?

The ice in the coffee can took longer to melt. The coffee can and the crumpled newspaper kept heat from the room away from the ice. The crumpled newspaper inside the coffee can trapped air, which is a good insulator. In your house you may have insulation made from fiberglass or plastic with trapped air pockets. Cellulose, the fibre in paper, is also used to make insulation.

DID YOU KNOW?

People have been insulating their homes for thousands of years. The ancient Egyptians used mud and papyrus. Ancient Greeks used cork from Spain to insulate their water pipes. In the Middle Ages people hung fabric tapestries on the walls to help keep rooms warm.

SQUARE TIRES

On really cold winter days, you might hear tires go "thunk, thunk, thunk." That's called having square tires. In this activity you'll find out how cold air can affect substances other than just water.

You Will Need
- 2 identical golf balls
- a freezer
- mittens or gloves
- 2 tennis balls

What to Do

1. Find a hard surface that you can use to bounce 2 golf balls. Hold the balls at chest height above the surface and let them both go at the same time. What happens?
2. Place one of the golf balls into the freezer for at least 2 hours. Take it out of the freezer using mittens or gloves.
3. Bounce the golf balls again as you did earlier. What happens now?
4. Try this experiment with different balls, such as tennis balls. Is there a difference?

WHAT HAPPENED?

The first time you bounced the golf balls they rose to the same height. The frozen ball didn't bounce as high. Balls bounce because they are elastic. They hit the floor, change shape slightly, then return to their original shape — just like if you stretch and let go of an elastic band. Cooling the balls makes them less elastic, so they bounce less. This effect is seen in different amounts with different types of balls. Tennis balls are elastic but are also filled with much more air than golf balls. That's why they bounced more. That's also why car tires make that sound. The cold air has taken up less room, making the tire flatter at the bottom.

TREAD SOFTLY

Look at your boots. Do they have thick bottoms or soles with zigzag designs? These "treads" are meant to help you grip the ground so you don't slide on the snow or ice. But what else might work if you didn't have boots?

You Will Need

- a helper
- a pair of winter boots
- a pair of flat or smooth soled shoes
- a pair of thick woollen socks

What to Do

1. Find an icy or snowy surface. Walk on the surface wearing your boots. Have your helper walk close beside you to catch you if you fall. Was it hard to walk on this surface?
2. Put a pair of fuzzy socks over a pair of shoes. Try walking on the icy or snowy surface wearing the socks. Was the ice slippery when you wore socks?
3. Now try walking on this surface wearing smooth-soled shoes. Make sure your helper is holding your hand so you don't fall.

WHAT HAPPENED?

Your thick, fuzzy socks kept you from slipping on the ice and snow. The socks acted much like the thick tread on your snow boots and provided **traction** or grip to the bottom of your feet by increasing the friction (a force that resists motion) between the boot and the ice surface. Flat or smooth soles allowed your feet to slide as there was nothing to stick or hold to the sole to the surface of the ice. The same principle applies to car tires. The tread or design of a tire is very important for drivers. In winter, cars need thick, deep treads to keep the car from sliding and to help the car drive through snow.

GLOSSARY

avalanche: a large amount of snow, rocks, and debris suddenly falling down a hill or mountainside

brine: a mixture of salt and water

calving: when a glacier releases a mass of ice to form an iceberg

cell: the smallest unit of a living thing capable of living on its own; all living things contain cells and can grow, reproduce and die

cryosphere: the parts of the Earth where water is frozen year-round

crystals: solids that are made of particles arranged in a regular repeating three dimensional pattern

freezing point: the temperature at which a pure substance changes from a liquid to a solid

frost: ice crystals that form when moist air makes contact with a freezing surface

frostbite: tissue damage caused by exposure to very cold temperatures

glaciers: long lasting sheets of ice and snow that form when more snow falls than melts each year

glaciologist: a scientist who study glaciers

ice core: a long tube of ice that is drilled from the ground in order to determine some of the atmospheric conditions at the time the snow fell

iceberg: an enormous floating piece of freshwater ice that has broken off of a glacier as it reaches the ocean

igloo: homes built with cut blocks of frozen snow

insulator: a material that prevents the transfer of heat

protein: a substance necessary for life that is found in all living things

refraction: the bending of light rays

quinzhee: an outdoor home made of snow, similar to a snow cave

snow blindness: a temporary eye irritation or blindness caused by the reflection of light off of snow

snowpack: the accumulation of snow which is packed and hardened under its own weight

terrain: an area of ground with its natural features

traction: the ability to move over a surface without slipping

water vapour: water in its gas state

wind chill: a temperature that represents how the current temperature and wind feels on exposed skin